Natural Energy

Jacqueline Dineen

Watts Books
London • New York • Sydney

Watts Books
96 Leonard Street
London EC2A 4RH

Franklin Watts Australia
14 Mars Road
Lane Cove
NSW 2060

UK ISBN: 0 7496 1448 X

10 9 8 7 6 5 4 3 2 1

Editor: Claire Llewellyn
Design: Caroline Ginesi
Artwork: Raymond Turvey
Cover artwork: Hugh Dixon
Picture research: Alison Renwick

A CIP catalogue record for this book is available from the British Library

Dewey Decimal Classification 333.79

Printed in Italy by G. Canale and C. SpA

Contents

New forms of energy

Most electricity is produced by burning coal, oil or gas to boil water to make steam which drives machinery. Coal, oil and gas are **fossil fuels**, which took millions of years to form. They will run out one day, so we need to find other ways of producing electricity. One method is to use natural **energy** sources such as the sun, wind and moving water.

▽ Power stations use fossil fuels, like coal, at an enormous rate. Within 100 years, there may be no fuel left.

Sources of natural energy

The sun, the wind and flowing water are renewable energy sources which will never run out. The heat of the sun can be used to make electricity. The power of water and the wind can drive machinery. Hot underground rocks provide heat called geothermal energy. These energy sources are all free. The problem is that they do not work to order.

▽ Everyone has felt the heat of the sun. Its energy can be stored to provide heat in the home. The panels on this roof collect the sun's energy to provide heat in this bath house.

We enjoy and make use of the power of the wind, but it does not always blow when we want it to.

Solar power

Solar power means 'power from the sun'. The simplest form of solar power is trapping sunlight to heat a greenhouse. Solar panels are now used to collect sunlight and store it for heating. Solar **cells** convert sunlight into electricity and are used on very different kinds of equipment, such as **satellites** and pocket calculators!

▷ Solar power provides the electricity needed by satellites as they circle the Earth.

▽ Solar cells provide enough energy to power these street lights in Israel.

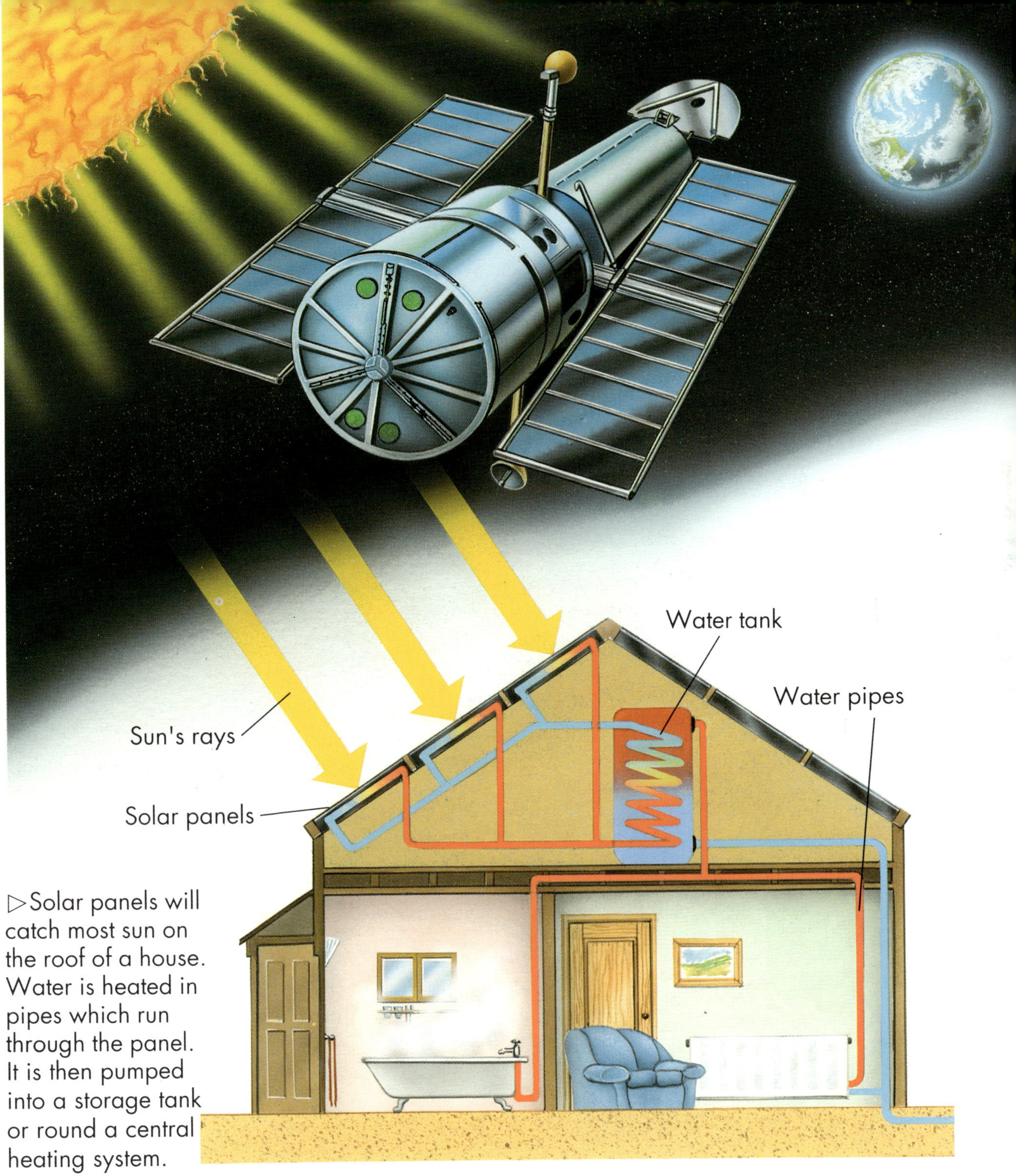

▷Solar panels will catch most sun on the roof of a house. Water is heated in pipes which run through the panel. It is then pumped into a storage tank or round a central heating system.

A solar power station

At a solar power station, huge mirrors are positioned to catch the sun as it moves across the sky. The sunlight is reflected on to a boiler. Enormous heat builds up and turns the water in the boiler into steam. The steam drives a machine called a **generator** which produces electricity.

▷ A solar power station in Albuquerque, New Mexico.

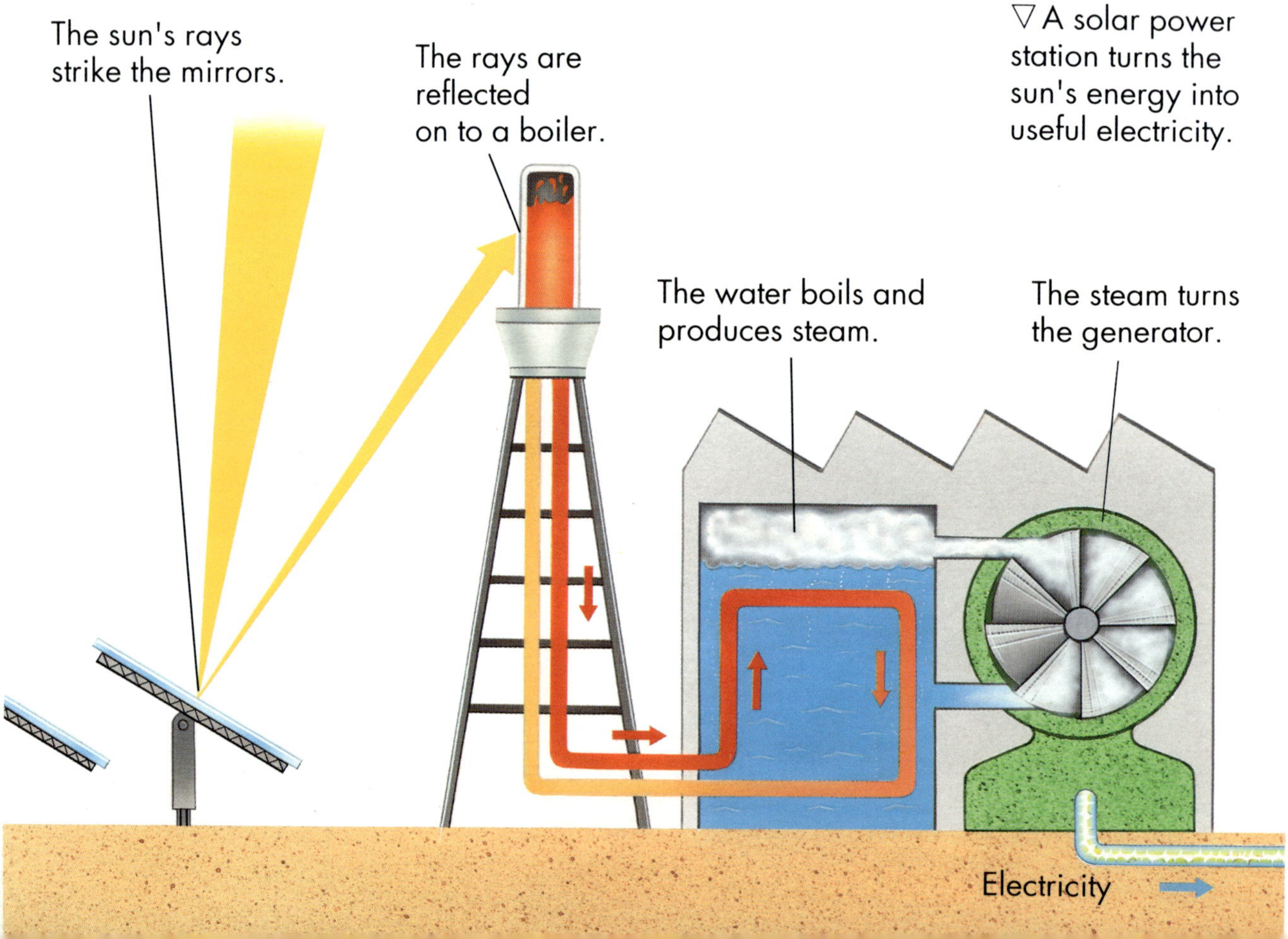

▽ A solar power station turns the sun's energy into useful electricity.

Wind power

People have used the power of the wind for centuries. Sailors learned that the wind blowing against the sail of a ship would push it through the water. By about 1150, people in Europe were using windmills to pump water and grind grain. As the wind turns the sails of a windmill, the sails turn a shaft which drives machinery inside the mill.

▽ Windmills are still used to pump flood water from low-lying land in the Netherlands. The canal carries the water away.

▷ This windmill is used to grind grain. The turning sails move a pole called a shaft. Machinery inside the mill turns the millstone which grinds the grain into flour.

On a wind farm

A wind **turbine** is a machine which uses the power of the wind to produce electricity. It is based on the same idea as the windmill, though it looks very different. The turbine has two or three blades and a tail vane to keep it turned into the wind. One turbine cannot produce much electricity. A wind farm is a group of turbines operating together.

▷ The spinning blades of the turbine turn a shaft inside the cabin. The shaft drives a generator which produces electricity.

▽ Wind farms are built in places where there is always plenty of wind, such as on cliffs and hilltops.

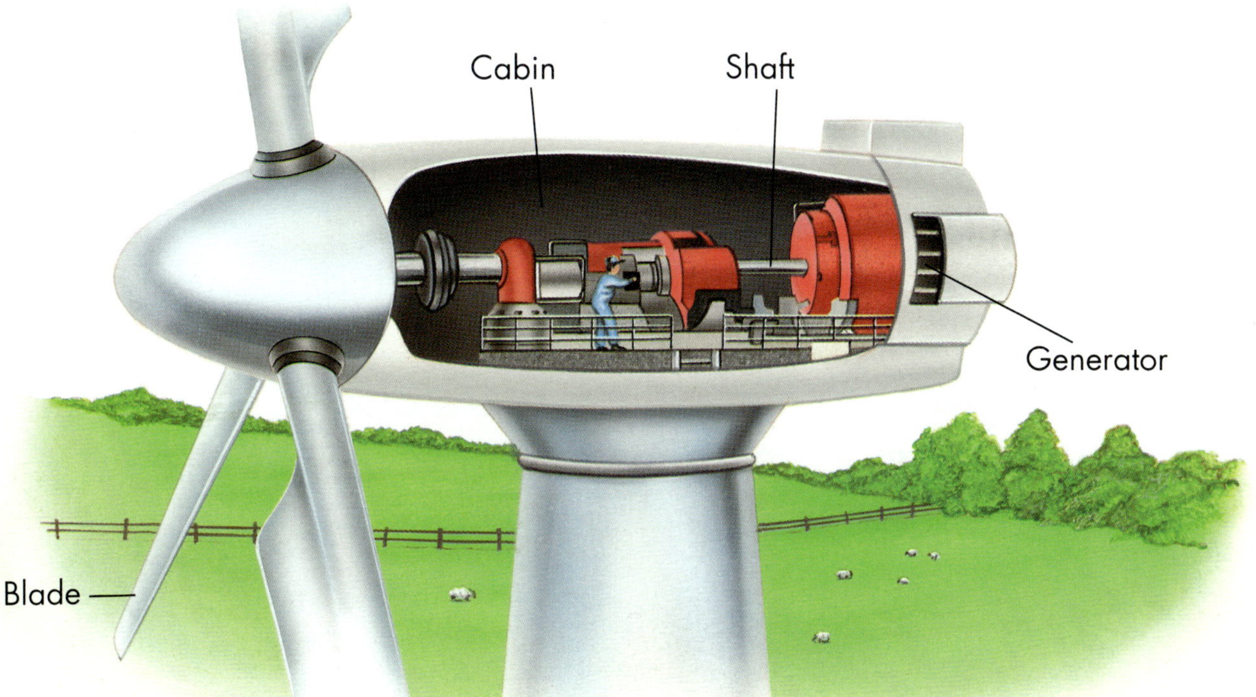

▽ Wind is stronger out at sea. Offshore wind farms are a possibility for the future.

Water power

▷ Water mills were built on the bank of a river.

A fast-flowing river has a lot of energy. People have been using water power to drive water wheels for about 2000 years. The water wheels were connected to machinery which turned millstones for grinding grain. Water wheels were also used to drive machinery in cloth mills and other factories.

◁ There are two types of water wheel. In the undershot wheel, the lower blades of the wheel are under the water. The flow of water pushes them round.

▷ In the overshot wheel, the water flows along a chute. It drops on to one paddle after another and turns the wheel round.

Hydro-electric power

Rushing water can be used to turn turbines and produce electricity. The water has to flow with great force. At a **hydro-electric** power station, a supply of water is stored behind a dam until a **reservoir** is formed. When the gates of the dam are opened, a powerful rush of water surges through huge tunnels and turns the turbines.

▷ When the gates in the dam are opened, water thunders down the tunnels and makes the turbines spin. The turbines drive generators which produce electricity.

▽ Hydro-electric power stations are built in mountainous areas where there are fast-flowing rivers.

Reservoir
Dam
Gate
Tunnel
Turbine
Generator

Tidal power

High and low tides in the sea are caused by the pull of **gravity** mainly from the Moon. Unlike other sources of natural energy, the tides are very reliable, and have been used to drive water mills for hundreds of years. Water is trapped in a millpond at high tide, and then let out when the tide has gone out. As it rushes out, the water turns a mill wheel.

▷ An ancient tidal mill in Essex.

▽ As the Moon moves round the Earth, its gravity pulls like a magnet.

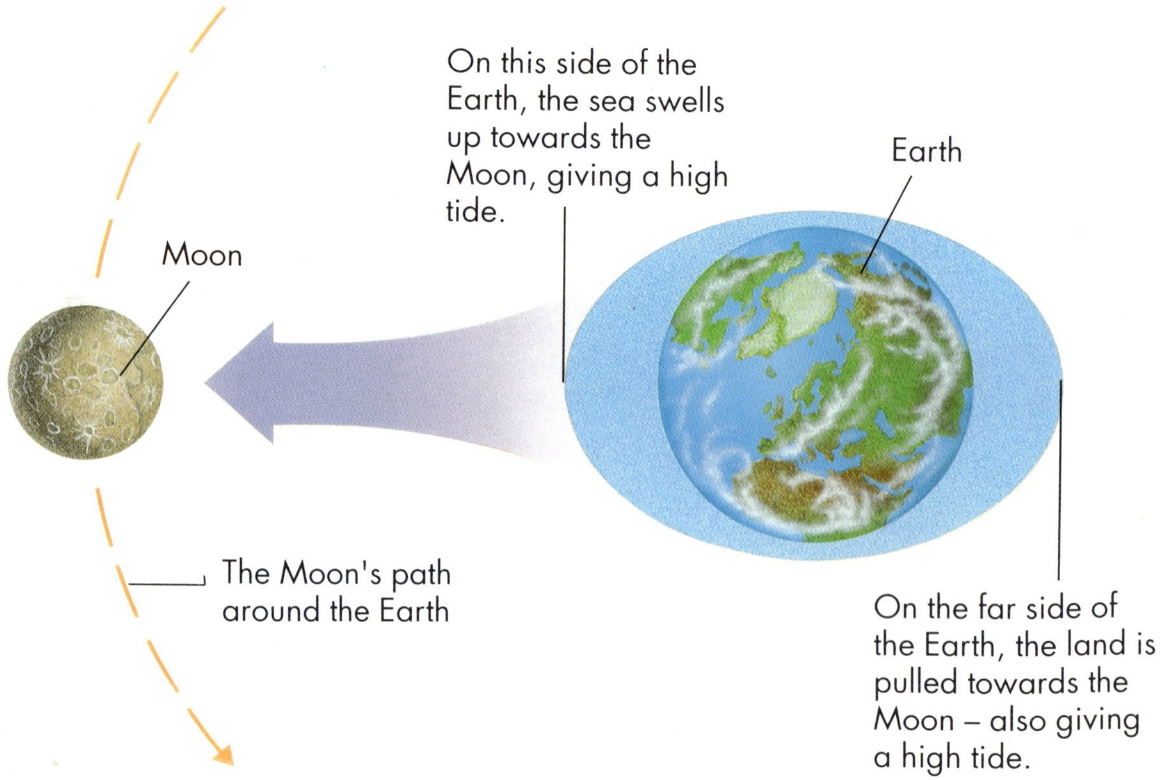

A tidal power station

Tidal power stations have to be built in places where there is a big difference between high and low tide. For example, in the Bay of Fundy in Canada, the water rises about 15 metres at high tide. Tidal power stations use the same method as tidal mills: water rushes to a lower level and turns a turbine as it does so. The turbine drives a generator.

▷ At high tide, water surges up through the open gates, turning the turbines. The gates close to trap the water.

▽ This tidal power station is at La Rance, in France.

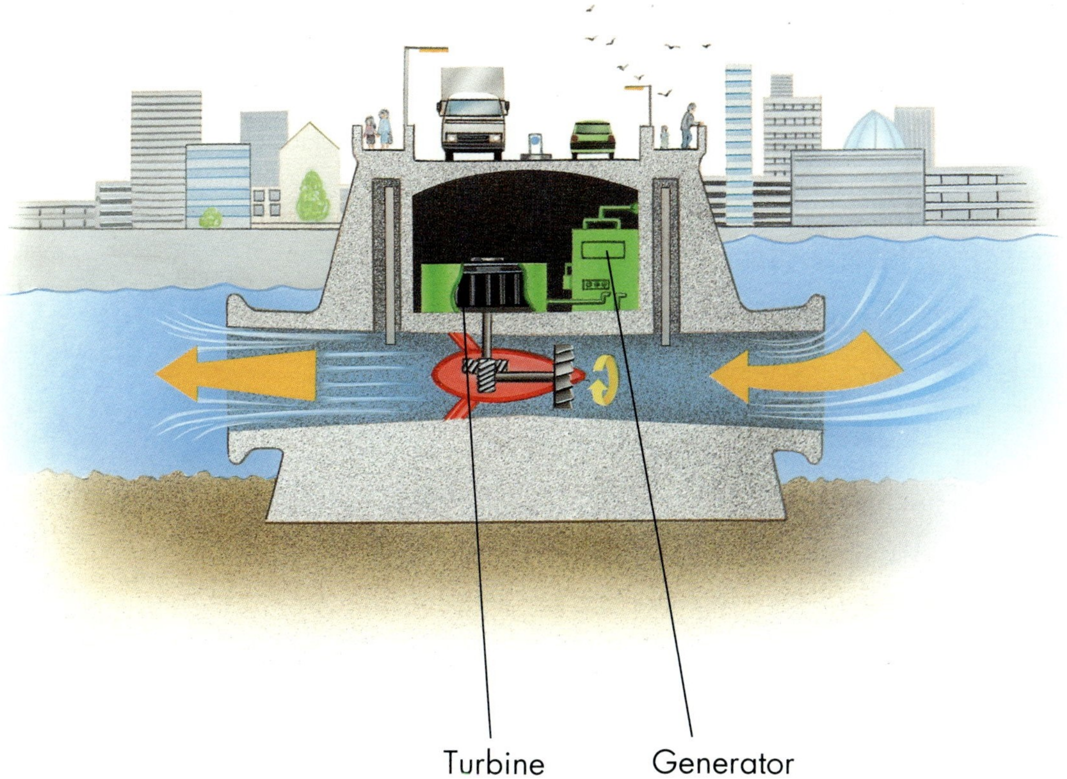

▷ At low tide, the gates are opened. The trapped water flows out towards the sea and turns the turbines.

Wave power

Waves are a very powerful source of natural energy. They are caused by the wind blowing across wide stretches of water far out at sea. When waves reach the coast, they batter the shore, and **erode** the rocks and cliffs. If this energy could be controlled properly, it could be used to produce electricity.

▷ Waves are especially powerful during a storm. They crash on to the beach with great force.

▽ The sea is so powerful, it can throw up damaged boats and huge tree trunks on to the shore.

Controlling the waves

Scientists are testing several different wave machines. They all use the up-and-down movement of waves to turn a turbine, and produce electricity. The best-known machine is the Salter Ducks. It has a row of floats which bob up and down on the waves. As they move, they pump powerful jets of water along a pipe, which then turn the blades of a turbine.

▷ This wave machine, called the 'Clam', uses the rise and fall of the waves to move air over a turbine.

▽ The Salter Ducks: as the floats bob up and down, their energy is used to generate electricity.

▽ Cockerell's Rafts are another kind of wave machine. As the rafts move, they pump air which turns a turbine.

Geothermal power

Heat can be trapped in rocks deep in the Earth. If water collects in these hot rocks, it heats up and shoots back to the surface as a hot water spring or as steam. The hot water or steam can be piped to a geothermal power station where it is used to drive a generator. This is known as geothermal energy.

▷ This hot spring, or geyser, is in New Zealand.

▽ Rainwater which has seeped down through soft rock may collect above a layer of hot hard rock. It may shoot up as steam or a hot spring.

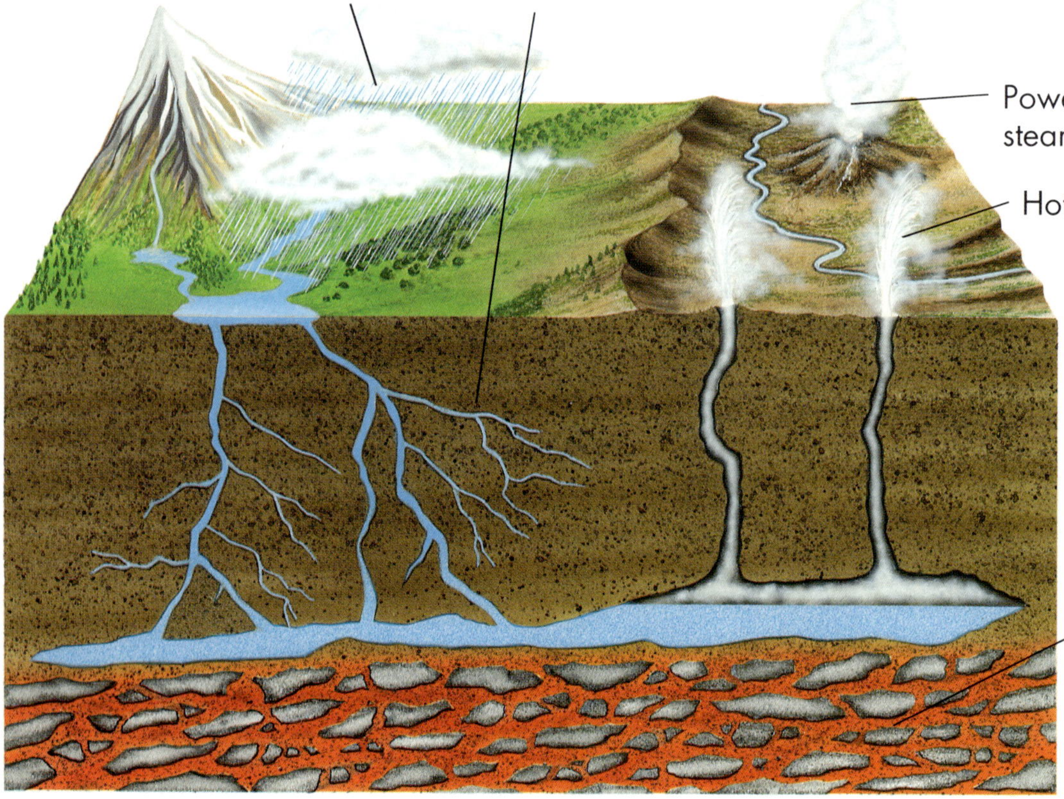

A geothermal power station

A geothermal power station makes use of underground heat to produce electricity. Two pipelines are drilled down to hot underground rocks. Water is pumped down, and changed into steam by the hot rocks. The steam shoots up a second pipe, driving the turbines in the power station above.

∇ Geothermal power stations are quite rare. This one is in Iceland. Others have been built in New Zealand, Australia, the USA and Japan.

▽In a geothermal power station, water is pumped down one hole, heated, and recovered as steam through another.

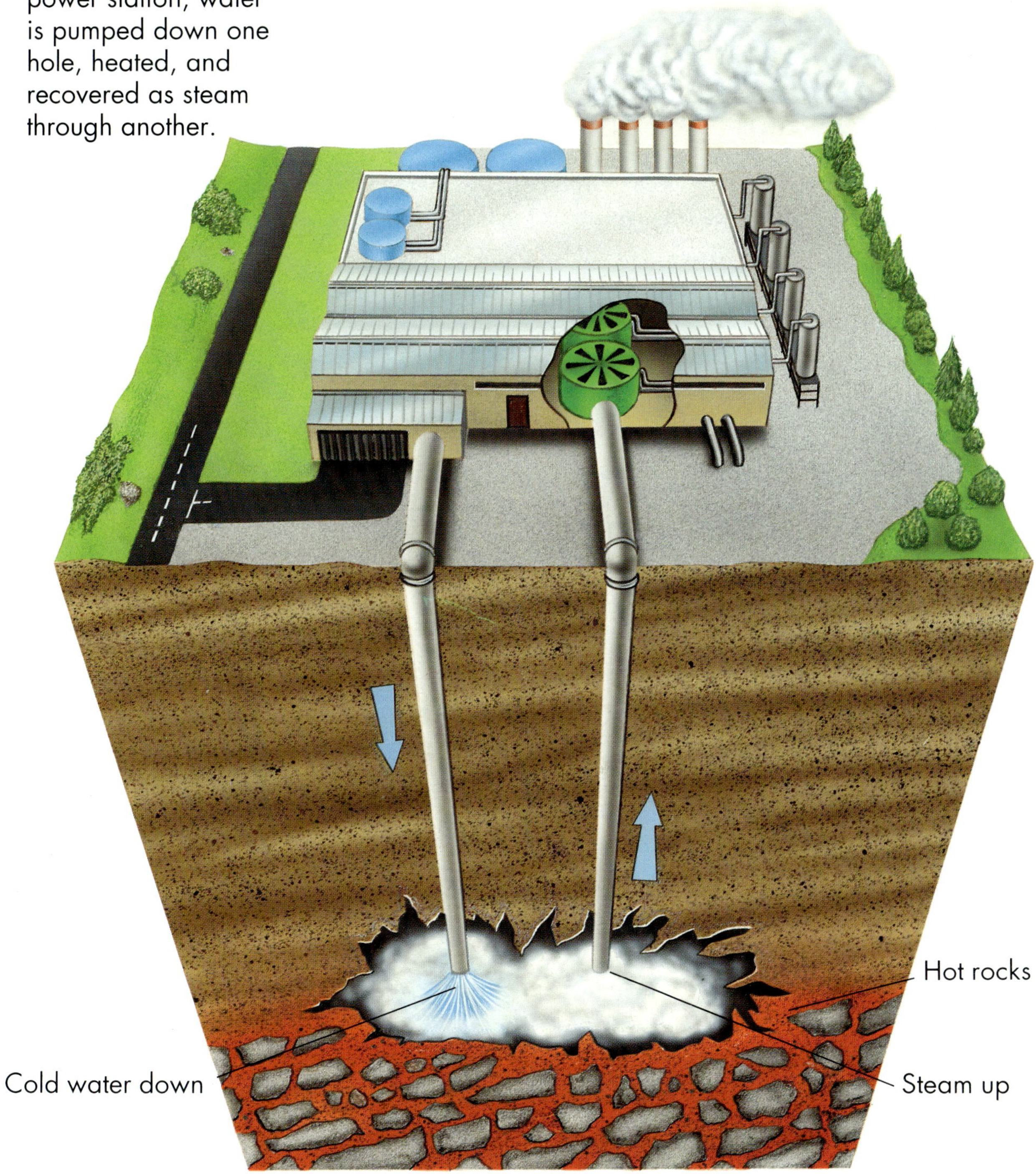

Things to do

- Did you know that bananas grow in Iceland? Find out how they are grown and which sort of energy is used.

- Design a solar-powered house. Which way should your house face to catch the most sunlight?

- Think of a good place to build a wind farm. Is there a suitable place near where you live?

Useful addresses:

Understanding Electricity
The Electricity Association
30 Millbank
London SW1P 4RD

Centre for Alternative Technology
Machynlleth
Powys SY20 9AZ

Glossary

atmosphere The layer of gases that surrounds the Earth.

cell A small unit for making electricity. A battery is a cell.

energy The power to do work and drive machines.

erode To wear away by wind or moving water.

fossil fuel A fuel made from the remains of animals and plants which died millions of years ago. Oil, gas and coal are fossil fuels.

generator A machine for producing electricity.

gravity The natural force or pull which pulls things together, such as the force between the Moon and the Earth.

hydro-electric Producing electricity by the power of falling water.

reservoir A place where a large amount of water is stored.

satellite A man-made object which circles the Earth to take pictures or send signals.

turbine The part of a generator or any engine which is made to turn by the force of pressure.

Index

Photographic credits:
J. Allan Cash 6, 14, 20; Martin Bond/Environmental Picture Library 3, 19; Martin Bond/Science Photo Library 25; Robert Harding Picture Library 10, 12, 23, 28; J. Holmes/ Environmental Picture Library 4; C. Jones/Environmental Picture Library 27; John Mead/Science Photo Library 16; Peter Menzel/ Science Photo Library 9.